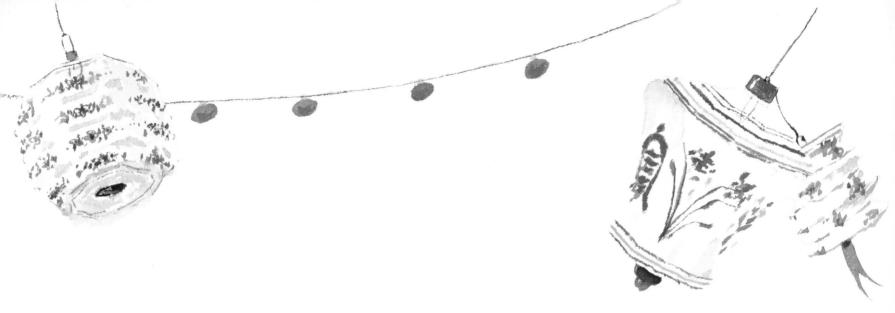

TEN GO TANGO

For my dancing family and friends—A.D.   For Lizzie Loughridge—E.A.M.

The art in this book was created using watercolor on Arches watercolor paper.

Ten Go Tango   Text copyright © 2000 by Arthur Dorros   Illustrations copyright © 2000 by Emily Arnold McCully
Printed in Hong Kong. All rights reserved.   Visit our web site at http://www.harperchildrens.com
Library of Congress Cataloging-in-Publication Data   Dorros, Arthur.
Ten go tango / by Arthur Dorros ; pictures by Emily Arnold McCully.   p.   cm.
Summary: In this counting book, ten groups of animals indulge in ten different dances,
from one osprey dancing ballet to ten flamingos doing the tango.   ISBN 0-06-027690-8. — ISBN 0-06-027691-6 (lib. bdg.)
[1. Animals—Fiction.   2. Dance—Fiction.   3. Counting.]   I. McCully, Emily Arnold, ill.   II. Title.   III. Title: 10 go tango.
PZ7.D7294Te   2000   98-5723   [E]—dc21   CIP   AC   Typography by Michele N. Tupper
1 2 3 4 5 6 7 8 9 10 ❖ First Edition

TEN GO TANGO

by Arthur Dorros · pictures by Emily Arnold McCully

HarperCollins*Publishers*

Here's the band—

they play

and play.

1

osprey

dances ballet.

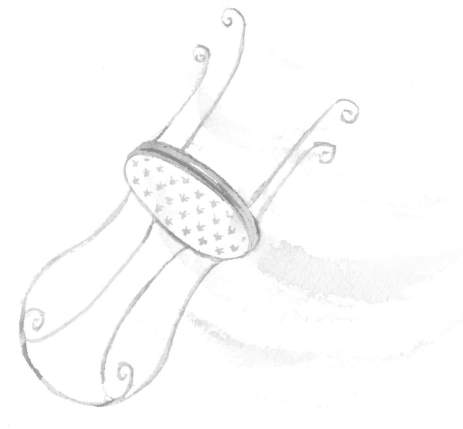

I spin, I leap.

2 **toucans**

can
two-step.

1 step,

2 steps.

3 bears

begin to cha-cha.

1, 2, 3,

cha,
cha,
cha.

4 foxes

surely fox-trot.

1 glides, 2 glide,

3 glide, 4.

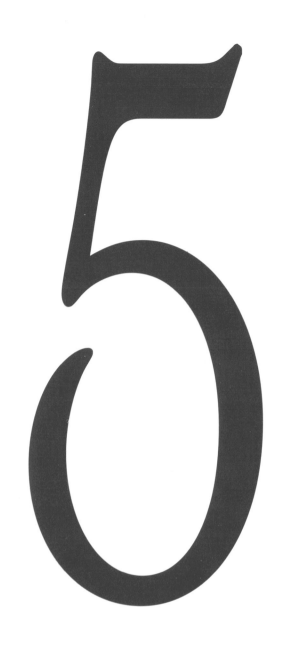

5

cats

tap dance.

Tap,

tap, tap, tap, tap,

5 are tapping.

crickets

jiggle jitterbug.

1 jiggles,

2 jiggle,

3 jiggle,

4,

5 jiggle,

6 jiggle

'cross the floor.

7 sheep

dance cancan. 1, 2, 3, lift.

way

up

high.

4 and 5, 6^{lift}, 7^{lift},

8 walruses

*start
to
waltz.*

*1 slides,
2 slide,*

3, 4, 5,

6, 7, 8,

slip
and
slide.

9 rhinos do the rumba.

1 bumps,

2 bump,

3 bump, 4, 5, 6, 7, 8, and 9,

rumble,

rumble,

rumble.

10 flamingos tango.

1 struts, 2 strut,

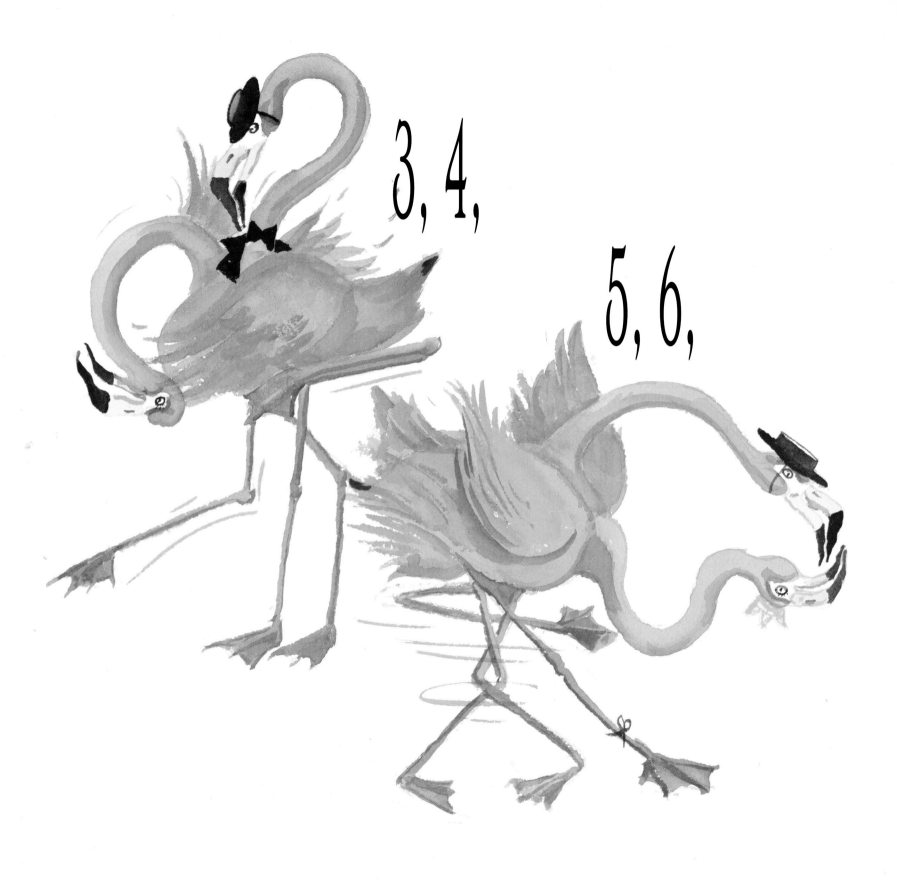

3, 4,

5, 6,

7 and 8 twirl,

9 and 10 twirl,

10 go tango!

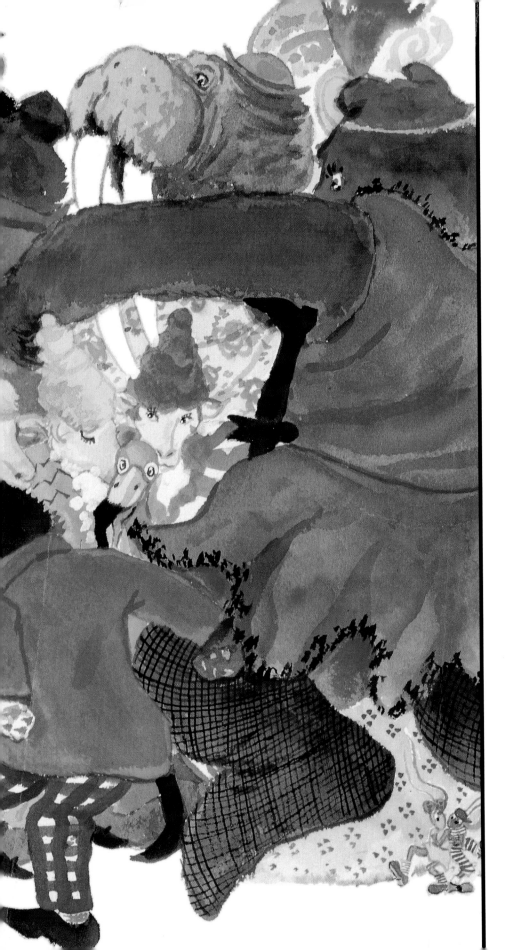

The floor
is shaking—

keep it
down!

We can't stop.
Let's dance
some more!

1 and 2 and 3 and 4!